Cryptocurrency

Day Trading Bitcoin, Ethereum, Gaming, and RWA Coins for Beginners—Building Your Path to Financial Freedom.

By Jim Peters

Cryptocurrency

CONTENTS

introduction 3

What Is Cryptocurrency.. 10

Is Cryptocurrency A Safe Investment? 12

Is Cryptocurrency Legal?... 15

Types Of Cryptocurrencies... 17

What Are Cryptocurrency Wallets? 19

Types Of Cryptocurrency Wallets 26

Why Invest In Crypto?.. 29

Essential Terminologies In Crypto 36

Why Crypto Is The Future Of Money Today?............ 106

Best Timing To Invest In Crypto 114

How To Buy Cryptocurrencies Today 125

   Making Your First Crypto Purchase: Step-By-Step Instructions 141

Conclusion... 146

INTRODUCTION

Check out the top cryptocurrencies with huge potential for big growth in 2025, including Bitcoin and Ethereum. As we step into a new phase of digital finance, investors are keen to find out which cryptos will dominate by 2025. With the market changing fast and tech innovations driving massive growth, the crypto space is ready for major transformations.

In this book, we'll dive into the key factors driving crypto growth in 2025 and share our top picks for coins with strong potential, along with some up-and-coming contenders you'll want to keep an eye on. In the next few years, crypto growth will depend on a mix of factors like market trends, adoption rates, new technology (like scalability and interoperability), government regulations, and the overall economy. How the market moves and how fast people adopt crypto are big drivers of its potential by 2025. As more people get interested in digital currencies, we're likely to see a huge jump in users—Crypto-Slate predicts there could be one billion crypto users by 2025.

Take Bitcoin, for example: it's quickly being adopted by merchants globally, and this trend is expected to keep growing. Merchant adoption could increase by about 50% in the next three years. As more businesses start accepting Bitcoin as payment, demand will rise, which could push the price up over time. Likewise, more interest from big institutional investors is boosting the overall crypto market.

Tech advancements are key to the future of cryptocurrencies and their potential for massive growth. As blockchain tech improves, we're seeing faster speeds, better scalability, stronger security, and more energy-efficient crypto networks.

For example, Bitcoin's 7 transactions per second (TPS.) and Ethereum's 30 TPS. show how innovations can push certain cryptos ahead in the race for mainstream adoption.

Government regulations are a major factor in how cryptocurrencies develop and grow. As countries worldwide figure out how to regulate this growing market, investors need to stay alert to how new laws might impact the value and adoption of different cryptos. Some countries are taking a stricter approach than others. In 2022, the U.S. government struggled to balance supporting crypto innovation while preventing illegal activities and financial instability.

Since the regulatory landscape is always changing, it can cause big shifts in certain crypto markets, and even create opportunities for some coins to thrive.

Cryptocurrency

A country's economic situation can seriously affect the growth and use of cryptocurrencies. Things like inflation, interest rates, unemployment, and government policies all play a part in shaping demand for digital currencies.

In places with shaky economies or where local currencies are losing value, cryptos can be a solid alternative for transactions. Venezuela is a perfect example—Bitcoin use shot up because of hyperinflation and the lack of trust in their national currency.

Bitcoin (BTC) is the first and biggest cryptocurrency, with a market cap currently over $600 billion. Launched in 2009 by an unknown creator using the name Satoshi Nakamoto, Bitcoin runs on a decentralized blockchain that allows secure, transparent transactions without banks or intermediaries.

Cryptocurrency

One reason BTC could see huge growth by 2025 is its limited supply—only 21 million Bitcoins will ever be available, which could drive up demand as more people and businesses adopt it. Plus, more institutional investors are starting to view Bitcoin as a valuable asset, putting money into it as a store of value.

Bitcoin (BTC) is the original and largest cryptocurrency, with a market cap topping $600 billion. It was introduced in 2009 by an anonymous creator known as Satoshi Nakamoto. Bitcoin operates on a decentralized blockchain, enabling secure and transparent transactions without needing banks or third parties.

One big reason BTC could see major growth by 2025 is its capped supply—only 21 million Bitcoins will ever exist, which could push demand higher as adoption increases.

Additionally, institutional investors are increasingly seeing Bitcoin as a solid store of value and are starting to invest in it.

To avoid losses and boost profits, it's crucial to factor in risk assessment, solid market research, diversification, and staying on top of the latest trends when investing in crypto. Cryptos are known for their volatility and lack of regulation, meaning prices can swing wildly in a short time, which could lead to losses.

Before putting any money into a cryptocurrency, make sure to do thorough research. Look into the project's technology, the team behind it, and its overall credibility. Also, it's smart to spread your investments across different digital assets to lower your overall risk. Keep a close watch on market trends and rely on trusted sources for your investment decisions.

Cryptocurrency

Before diving into crypto investments, it's important to do thorough research on potential options. If you're just starting out, begin by understanding different cryptocurrencies and their uses.

For instance, Ethereum is popular for its smart contracts, which enable decentralized apps to be built on its platform.

Keeping up with market trends and volatility is also key. You can stay informed by reading news or joining online crypto communities to discuss market movements.

Remember, digital assets are more volatile than traditional investments like stocks or bonds, so always factor in the risks before committing your money.

WHAT IS CRYPTOCURRENCY

Cryptocurrencies are digital currencies backed by cryptographic systems, allowing for secure online payments without needing a middleman. The "crypto" part refers to the encryption methods, like elliptical curve encryption, public-private key pairs, and hashing, that protect these transactions.

The key technology behind Bitcoin and other cryptos is the blockchain. A blockchain is basically a series of connected data blocks stored on an online ledger. Each block holds a group of transactions that are independently verified by validators across the network. Each new block created must be verified before it's confirmed, making it nearly impossible to fake transaction histories. The online ledger is maintained by a network of nodes (computers), and they all have to agree on its contents.

Experts believe blockchain tech has the potential to be useful in various industries, including supply chains, online voting, and crowdfunding. Even big financial players like JPMorgan Chase & Co. are using blockchain to cut transaction costs and simplify payment processing.

Is Cryptocurrency a Safe Investment?

Cryptocurrencies have a reputation for being risky, mainly because of scams, hacks, bugs, and extreme price swings. Even though the technology behind it, like blockchain, is secure, using and storing crypto can be tricky, especially for beginners.

Besides the usual market risks with speculative assets, crypto investors should keep these risks in mind:

User risk: Crypto transactions can't be reversed or canceled once sent. It's estimated that about 20% of all Bitcoins are lost forever due to forgotten passwords or sending to the wrong address.

Regulatory risk: In many places, the legal status of crypto is still unclear. Governments might regulate it as securities or currency, and sudden changes could make it hard to sell or cause prices to crash.

Counterparty risk: Many people rely on exchanges or third parties to store their crypto. If these services get hacked or go under, you could lose everything.

Management risk: Without strong regulations, there are few safeguards against dishonest or bad management practices. Many investors have lost money because of teams that didn't deliver on promises.

Programming risk: Some platforms use smart contracts to manage user funds. If there's a bug or vulnerability in the code, investors might lose their deposits.

Market manipulation: Manipulation is a big problem in the crypto world, with powerful individuals, organizations, or exchanges acting unethically to influence prices.

Cryptocurrency

Despite these risks, the total market cap of cryptocurrencies has skyrocketed to around $2.4 trillion, and some early investors have made significant profits by taking the risk of investing early.

Is Cryptocurrency Legal?

Unlike traditional money, which gets its authority from governments (like the U.S. dollar being official legal tender), cryptocurrencies aren't backed by any government or central bank. Because of this, it's been tricky for different countries to agree on their legal status, and crypto mostly operates outside regular financial systems.

In the U.S., the legal standing of cryptocurrencies affects how they're used in trading and transactions. In June 2019, the Financial Action Task Force (FATF) suggested that crypto transfers should follow its Travel Rule, meaning they must comply with anti-money laundering (AML) rules.

Even though crypto can act like money, the IRS treats it as an asset or property for taxes. Just like with other investments, if you make a profit by

Cryptocurrency

selling or trading crypto, you'll owe taxes. Whether it's taxed as capital gains or regular income depends on how long you held the cryptocurrency and how you used it.

TYPES OF CRYPTOCURRENCIES

There are many types of cryptocurrencies, each created to support specific tasks on the blockchain they're built on. For example, Ethereum's ether (ETH) was made to pay for transaction validation and block creation. After Ethereum switched to proof-of-stake in September 2022, ether also became the blockchain's staking token. Similarly, XRP, from the XRP Ledger Foundation, is designed to help financial institutions move funds across borders.

With so many cryptocurrencies out there, it's important to understand their purpose. Coins with a clear use case are usually less risky to invest in compared to those without a defined function.

When people talk about cryptocurrencies, they often mention the coin's name, but it's useful to know the different types as well. Here are a few common types of cryptocurrencies and examples of tokens in each category:

Platform Tokens: These are used to support apps running on a blockchain, like Solana.

Security Tokens: These represent ownership of real-world assets that have been tokenized, such as MS Token, which gives partial ownership of the Millennium Sapphire.

Utility Tokens: Examples include XRP and ETH, which have specific functions on their blockchains.

Transactional Tokens: These are created to be used as payment methods, with Bitcoin being the most famous.

Governance Tokens: These give holders voting rights on a blockchain, like Uniswap.

What are Cryptocurrency Wallets?

A cryptocurrency wallet is a secure digital tool that lets you manage your crypto assets. With it, you can send, receive, and trade different cryptocurrencies. Crypto itself is a type of digital currency that's secured by cryptography and operates on decentralized blockchain networks.

Some wallets support multiple coins like Bitcoin, Ethereum, Litecoin, Ripple, and Dogecoin, while others are designed for just one type of crypto. The key thing to remember is that only you, the wallet owner, have access to your funds—no one else can touch them.

Cryptocurrency wallets don't actually hold your blockchain assets. Instead, they store your public and private keys, which prove you own the crypto and allow you to make transactions. Your public key points to your crypto's address on the blockchain and is what you share when receiving payments. The private key, unique to your wallet, is never shared and is needed to send or manage your crypto.

Some wallets come with extra features like signing keys for identification, executing smart contracts, or signing digital documents.

Businesses also use crypto wallets to accept payments through cryptocurrency gateways for their products and services.

When you set up some wallets, you can create a "seed" phrase—a long phrase that's an unencrypted version of your private key. If you lose access to your wallet, the seed phrase lets you recover it, along with your keys and crypto.

For extra protection, some wallets use multi-signature (multi-sig) security, which means two or more keys are needed to approve a transaction. These keys can be held by different people or stored on separate devices, like a mobile app and an offline hardware wallet.

A custodial wallet, also called a hosted wallet, is offered by crypto exchanges. When you buy crypto, the exchange holds your private keys and manages the funds in their wallet until you withdraw them, making storage and security their responsibility.

Before choosing a cryptocurrency wallet, consider these factors:

Use Case: If you're using crypto to pay for goods and services, go with a hot wallet that's either mobile or cloud-based. If security is your priority, a hardware wallet is a better fit. For long-term investments, cold wallets (either hardware or paper) are ideal. Hardware wallets are great for long-term storage, while paper wallets are often used for holding large amounts of crypto.

Cryptocurrency Assets: Many exchanges suggest a wallet, and you can use their custodial services if you prefer. If you hold multiple cryptos, make sure the wallet supports all your assets since not all multi-crypto wallets cover every coin.

Wallet Pricing: Wallets can cost up to $200 or more, especially hardware ones. Some wallets are free. Depending on the transaction, you might also pay a flat fee or a percentage of the transaction amount.

What do Cryptocurrency Wallets do?

Cryptocurrency wallets are used to store, send, and receive crypto. They hold your public and private keys, which prove ownership of your digital assets and enable transactions.

Benefits of Using Cryptocurrency Wallets:

Convenience: Online wallets make it easy to use crypto for payments or receive funds from anywhere in the world.

Cost: Lower transaction fees compared to traditional banks.

Security: They protect your private keys.

Balance Monitoring: Easily track your crypto holdings.

How Much Do Cryptocurrency Wallets Cost?

Wallets can cost up to $200 or more, depending on the type. Some are free, but there may be flat fees or a percentage charged on transactions.

What Are the Best Cryptocurrency Wallets?

Here are some of the most popular wallets on the market:

Here are a few well-known cryptocurrency wallets:

COINOMI

COINSBANK

UBERPAY

BITGO

EXODUS

JAXX LIBERTY

COINBASE WALLET

TREZOR

These wallets are widely used for managing crypto assets, providing different features depending on your needs.

TYPES OF CRYPTOCURRENCY WALLETS

Software Wallets (also known as hot wallets/storage) are connected to the internet, with keys stored in an app or software. You can access them through the cloud, mobile apps, or desktop programs. These wallets let you manage all your crypto in one place, control your private keys, send/receive crypto globally, use usernames instead of long addresses, and shop where crypto is accepted. However, they're more exposed to hacks and viruses.

Hardware Wallets store your keys on a USB drive, which you need to plug into your computer to access your crypto.

Paper Wallets have your keys printed on paper, often as a QR code for easy access.

Hardware and paper wallets, also called cold wallets, are usually offline, making them more private and less likely to get hacked. However, they can be lost or damaged, and they aren't as easy to use as other options.

These are non-custodial wallets, meaning you control your private keys and crypto. You're responsible for keeping track of your keys and securing them. If you lose access to your private keys, you'll permanently lose access to your funds.

Key Features of Cryptocurrency Wallets

A good crypto wallet should offer most or all of these features:

- Store public and private keys on software, hardware, or paper, depending on the wallet type.

- Connect to blockchain networks to store, send, receive, and trade cryptocurrencies.

- Monitor your balance.

- Support multiple cryptocurrencies.

- Include security measures to ensure only the wallet owner has access to private keys.

- Support for signing transactions.

- Available as cloud-based, mobile apps, desktop software, USB/flash drives, or paper, based on the wallet type.

Why Invest in Crypto?

There's no denying the explosive growth of digital currencies. Fueled by the success of Bitcoin (BTC) and Ethereum (ETH), the cryptocurrency space keeps expanding.

Beyond just initial coin offerings (ICOs), there are now many new blockchain-based investment options, from decentralized finance (DeFi) to non-fungible tokens (NFTs). Many crypto enthusiasts believe these investments could create the next wave of digital millionaires (or even billionaires). But if you haven't invested in crypto yet, you might be wondering if now's the time to jump in. Let's look at some reasons people invest in crypto and what to consider before you do.

Cryptocurrencies are often seen as a game-changing technology with the potential to revolutionize various industries. Since they can't be printed or seized, they could also serve as a secure store of value. However, it's important to remember that crypto is still highly speculative, and there's no certainty it will ever become widely adopted. Before diving in, make sure to follow the necessary security protocols carefully. Another reason people invest in cryptocurrency is for a stable, long-term store of value. Unlike fiat currencies, many cryptocurrencies have a fixed supply, limited by mathematical algorithms. This means governments or political entities can't reduce their value through inflation. Plus, because of the cryptographic nature of crypto, it's impossible for a government to tax or seize tokens without the owner's consent.

While many believe digital currencies could eventually become part of everyday life, the crypto market is currently driven by speculative trading. Studies show that most blockchain activity involves exchange trades, which far outweigh regular transactions or purchases. High-profile skeptics like Warren Buffett, Bill Gates, and JPMorgan CEO JAMIE DIMON have all warned of a possible crypto bubble.

Cryptocurrencies aren't the only asset subject to speculative manias—markets like cannabis stocks, tech stocks, precious metals, and real estate have also seen bubbles that ended badly for some investors.

As a new technology, speculative behavior in crypto is expected, especially as blockchain develops. However, new investors should be cautious of falling into traps like herd mentality, Fear of Missing Out (FOMO), or the Greater Fool Fallacy, which can mean the difference between a smart risk and a poor decision.

Is Investing in Crypto Worth It?

Whether crypto is a good investment depends on your personal financial situation. If you're thinking about adding it to your portfolio, it's smart to talk to a financial advisor to discuss your goals and how much risk you're comfortable with.

How Do I Start Investing in Crypto?

First, research the cryptocurrency and its blockchain project to understand its purpose. Check how it's used, recent developments, price trends, trading volume, and market cap. You can then open an account on a crypto exchange and start investing. Alternatively, you could invest in a cryptocurrency exchange-traded fund (ETF) through a brokerage, which is usually more affordable and doesn't require you to handle the crypto yourself. A financial advisor with knowledge of crypto can help you decide if it's right for your portfolio.

Which Crypto Is Best to Invest in Now?

That depends on your goals, risk tolerance, and view of the market. Before investing, it's best to consult with a financial advisor to see if a specific cryptocurrency aligns with your investment strategy.

While there are plenty of reasons to be cautious about digital currencies, many traditional investors have embraced this new asset class. The blockchain industry is often compared to the internet in the 1990s, with the potential to revolutionize multiple sectors.

However, crypto enthusiasts need to be aware of the risks before diving in. Along with learning the necessary security protocols and researching their investments, they should also take time to understand the common mistakes that often trip up beginners in the crypto space.

Thefts and Other Risks

One of cryptocurrency's biggest strengths—its decentralized nature—also creates major risks. Without a central authority, it's up to users to securely store the cryptographic keys that control their funds. For investors in crypto, it's essential to follow strict security measures, though even these might not fully protect against hackers, who are always improving their techniques.

Theft is a constant threat in the crypto world, with hackers stealing billions from exchanges, wallets, and users. Scams like doubling schemes, social engineering, market manipulation, and fake ICOs also target unsuspecting users.

A big risk also comes from the users themselves. Most crypto wallets can't be reset if you forget your passphrase. Many have lost millions in crypto

Cryptocurrency

simply due to forgotten passwords or misplaced devices.

ESSENTIAL TERMINOLOGIES IN CRYPTO

Address Delegation

When you let a Super STAKER handle your wallet's stake for you.

Airdrop

A marketing method where free tokens are handed out to traders to boost interest in a cryptocurrency.

Algorithm

A set of steps or rules designed to solve a problem or carry out a task.

Algorithmic Stablecoin

These are tokens that stay pegged to a currency (usually the U.S. dollar) by following rules in software, no physical assets involved.

All-Time-High (ATH)

The highest price or market value a cryptocurrency has ever hit.

All-Time-Low (ATL)

The lowest price or market value a cryptocurrency has ever dropped to.

Altcoin

Any cryptocurrency that isn't Bitcoin.

Application Programming Interface (API)

A software bridge that lets two different applications or platforms talk to each other and share data.

Application-Specific Integrated Circuit (ASIC)

Specialized computers designed to perform one task, like solving the puzzles for Bitcoin's Proof-of-Work system.

Arbitrage

A trading method where you buy cryptocurrency at a lower price in one market and sell it for a higher price in another, pocketing the difference.

ASIC Resistant

This refers to cryptocurrencies with Proof-of-Work systems that are built in a way that prevents ASICs from having an advantage over regular consumer hardware.

Ask Me Anything (AMA)

A Q&A session where people from a certain field (like a CEO or expert) answer questions from the public.

Atomic Swap

A direct trade between cryptocurrencies on different blockchains without needing a middleman.

Automatic Replay Protection

A security feature in Bitcoin Cash that helps prevent replay attacks, where transactions might be duplicated.

Bag-holder

Someone holding a large amount of a cryptocurrency that's losing value or has become worthless.

BAKKT

A company set up by the Intercontinental Exchange (owner of the New York Stock Exchange) to offer cryptocurrency futures and options.

Batch Auction

An auction that distributes tokens to participants based on how much they contribute to the pool.

Bearish

A negative outlook on the market or asset, expecting prices to drop.

Bear Market

A market trend where prices are generally falling, opposite of a bull market.

Bitcoin ATM

A machine where you can buy or sell Bitcoin and sometimes other cryptocurrencies.

Bitcoin Evangelist

Someone who is very enthusiastic about Bitcoin and spends time promoting and educating others about it.

Bitcoin Improvement Proposal (BIP)

Suggestions for upgrades or new features to the Bitcoin network.

Bit-License

A license that companies in New York need if they're dealing with cryptocurrencies, issued by the New York State Department of Financial Services.

Block

A collection of transaction data that is added to the blockchain, forming a new link in the chain.

Blockchain

Bitcoin's public, decentralized ledger where all transaction data is recorded.

Block Confirmation

The number of blocks added after a specific block, showing how secure that block is.

Block Explorer

An online tool that lets you view details about transactions or blocks on a blockchain.

Block Height

The number that shows the position of a block in the blockchain.

Block Reward

The reward given to miners or validators for adding a new block to the blockchain.

Bloodbath

A situation where the market is crashing, and many assets are rapidly losing value.

Bots

Programs that automatically execute trades based on set conditions.

Bounty

A reward offered for completing certain tasks.

BUIDL

Advice to actively contribute to the blockchain ecosystem rather than just waiting for price increases.

Bullish

A positive outlook on the market or asset, expecting prices to rise.

Bull Market

A market trend where prices are generally rising.

Burned Tokens

Tokens that have been sent to an address with no known private key, making them unusable.

Buy/Sell Tax

A fee that's taken when tokens are bought or sold, which is sent to a designated address.

Buy Wall

A very large buy order placed at a single price point, creating a "wall" in the order book.

Byzantine Fault

When something goes wrong in a system but it can't figure out which component failed, leading to continued errors.

Byzantine Generals' Problem

A situation where a group needs to agree on a strategy, but they can't trust each other or communicate reliably.

cc0 NFT

An NFT where the creator has given up all intellectual property rights.

Central Bank Digital Currency (CBDC)

A digital version of a country's fiat currency, issued by its central bank, unlike cryptocurrencies issued by non-governmental entities.

Centralized

A system where control is in the hands of a few individuals or entities.

Central Ledger

A central database used by a bank or company to store records.

Circulating Supply

The total number of coins or tokens available for trading in the market.

Cloud Mining

Mining cryptocurrencies using rented processing power from companies that host the physical machines.

Cold Storage

Keeping your cryptocurrency offline, which is considered safer because it requires physical access to use.

Cold Wallet

A wallet that is kept offline and needs physical access, like a hardware wallet.

Collateralized Debt Obligation (CDO)

A complex financial product based on the value of underlying assets, usually sold to institutional investors.

Composability

The ability to combine different parts of a software stack to build more complex systems.

Consensus

When all participants in a blockchain agree on the next block to be added.

Crowd-sale

A type of sale where tokens are sold at a fixed price on a first-come, first-serve basis.

Crypto Bubble

A period of speculation where cryptocurrency prices skyrocket before crashing.

Cryptography

The practice of converting readable information into a secure format that can only be deciphered by those with the right knowledge.

Custody

The protection or guardianship of an asset.

Daily Active Addresses (DAA)

Refers to the number of blockchain addresses that meet the criteria for activity within a day.

Dead Cat Bounce

A brief price recovery after a prolonged decline, followed by further losses.

Decentralized

A system with no central authority or single point of failure.

Decentralized Applications (DAPPS)

Apps running on peer-to-peer networks like Ethereum without a central authority.

Decentralized Autonomous Organization (DAO)

Open-source systems that operate without centralized control.

Decentralized Finance (DeFi)

A movement focused on building financial applications without central authorities.

Decryption

The process of turning encrypted data back into its original, readable form.

Degen

Crypto trading without proper research—essentially gambling.

Delegated Proof-of-Stake (DPOS)

A consensus mechanism where elected delegates validate transactions and produce blocks.

Derivatives

Financial instruments whose value is based on the performance of an underlying asset (e.g., gold, oil).

Derivatives Market

The market where derivatives like futures and options are traded.

Difficulty

A measure of how hard it is to correctly guess a new block in blockchain mining.

Directed Acyclic Graph (DAG)

A data structure that moves in one direction and never repeats.

Distributed Denial of Service (DDoS) Attack

A cyber-attack that overwhelms a network with traffic to disrupt services.

Distributed Ledger

A ledger where data is stored across a network of nodes.

Distributed Ledger Technology (DLT)

The technology behind distributed ledgers.

Dominance

Refers to Bitcoin's share of the overall market capitalization.

Double Spending

The act of spending the same digital currency twice, often through fraudulent means.

Do Your Own Research (DYOR)

Advice for investors to conduct their own research before investing.

Dump

A term used to describe a market decline or the act of selling holdings.

Dusting Attack

A technique where scammers send tiny amounts of crypto to track users and potentially break their anonymity.

Dutch Auction

An auction that starts with a high price, which gradually decreases until it hits a set floor price.

EIP (Ethereum Improvement Proposal)

A proposal for updates or new features on the Ethereum network.

Emission

The rate at which new coins are created and released, as per the protocol.

Encryption

The process of encoding data using an algorithm to protect its confidentiality.

Enterprise Ethereum Alliance (EEA)

A group of Ethereum developers and businesses collaborating to use Ethereum for business applications.

ERC-1155

A token standard on Ethereum that allows for both fungible and non-fungible tokens.

ERC-20

A widely-used Ethereum token standard for creating fungible tokens.

ERC-721

An Ethereum token standard for creating non-fungible tokens (NFTs).

Ethereum Name Service (ENS)

A lookup service that allows users to send and receive funds using simple names instead of long addresses.

Ethereum Virtual Machine (EVM)

The runtime environment where Ethereum smart contracts are executed.

Exchange-Traded Fund (ETF)

A security that tracks a group of assets, such as stocks or cryptocurrencies, and trades like a single stock.

Explain Like I'm Five (ELI5)

To explain a concept in such simple terms that even a child could understand.

Externally Owned Accounts (EOA)

Ethereum accounts controlled by private keys, with no associated code.

Faucet

A website or app that rewards users with small amounts of cryptocurrency over time.

Fear of Missing Out (FOMO)

The fear that missing out on an investment opportunity could lead to regret later.

Fear, Uncertainty, and Doubt (FUD)

A strategy of spreading false or misleading information to discourage crypto investment.

Fiat-Pegged Cryptocurrency

Cryptos that are tied to the value of a traditional asset, such as a fiat currency.

FLAPPENING

When Litecoin overtakes Bitcoin Cash in value or size, inspired by the term "Flippening" (when another crypto overtakes Bitcoin).

FRONTRUN

Intercepting a large order on a decentralized exchange to make a quick profit.

Full Node

A computer that verifies and enforces the rules of a given blockchain.

Full Pay-Per-Share (FPPS)

Similar to PPS, but includes an additional transaction fee incentive for identifying a block.

Fully Diluted Valuation (FDV)

The hypothetical market cap of a cryptocurrency if all its supply were in circulation, based on the current price.

Futures

Contracts that oblige two parties to transact in the future, based on terms set in advance.

Gas

A unit measuring the computational effort required for transactions or smart contracts on Ethereum.

Gas Limit

The maximum amount of gas a user is willing to spend on an Ethereum transaction.

Gas Price

The amount a user is willing to pay for gas to execute a transaction on Ethereum.

Genesis Block

The very first block in a blockchain, often referred to as 'block 0' or 'block 1.'

Goblin Town

A term for a prolonged market downtrend, similar to a bear market.

Golden Cross

A bullish chart pattern where the short-term moving average crosses above the long-term moving average.

Graphical Processing Unit (GPU)

A chip designed for graphics processing that can also be used for cryptocurrency mining.

GWEI

A denomination of Ether used to measure gas prices.

Halving

An event that cuts the mining rewards for Proof-of-Work miners by half, reducing the supply of new coins.

Hard Cap

The maximum amount of funds an Initial Coin Offering (ICO) aims to raise.

Hard Fork

A permanent split in a blockchain resulting in two separate chains that no longer recognize each other.

Hash

A unique alphanumeric code produced by a hash function from an input string.

HASHGRAPH

A distributed ledger technology similar to blockchain, considered its potential successor.

HASHRATE

The total computing power used by miners in a blockchain network.

HODL

A slang term in crypto meaning to hold onto assets rather than selling them.

Hot Wallet

A cryptocurrency wallet that's always connected to the internet.

Hybrid PoW/POS

A consensus model that combines Proof-of-Work and Proof-of-Stake mechanisms on the same network.

Hyperledger (Hyperledger Foundation)

An open-source project to develop blockchain technologies, hosted by the Linux Foundation.

IEO (Initial Exchange Offering)

A fundraising model where token sales are conducted on a crypto exchange rather than by the token's creators.

Immutable

A characteristic of blockchain data that cannot be changed once recorded.

Impermanent Loss

A temporary loss experienced by liquidity providers due to price divergence between token pairs.

Initial Coin Offering (ICO)

A fundraising method where a company or project raises funds by selling new cryptocurrency tokens.

Internet of Things (IoT)

A system allowing internet-connected devices to communicate without human intervention.

Interoperability

The ability of different systems or blockchains to work together without restrictions.

Inter-Planetary File System (IPFS)

A peer-to-peer protocol for storing and sharing files in a distributed network.

IPO (Initial Public Offering)

The process of offering shares of a company to the public for the first time to raise capital.

IYKYK (If You Know, You Know)

A phrase used to imply insider knowledge that only certain people will understand.

Kimchi Premium

The price difference of Bitcoin between South Korean exchanges and global markets.

KYC (Know Your Customer)

A process requiring businesses to verify the identity of their clients.

Ledger

A record of financial transactions that is permanent and cannot be altered.

Leverage

Borrowing funds to increase the potential return of an investment.

Lightning Network

A second-layer payment protocol on top of a blockchain that enables instant transactions without needing block confirmation.

Limit Order / Limit Buy / Limit Sell

Orders set by traders to buy or sell crypto at a specific price.

Liquidity

The ease with which a cryptocurrency can be bought or sold without affecting the market price.

Liquid Proof of Stake (LPOS)

A Proof-of-Stake system used by TEZOS, slightly different from Delegated Proof-of-Stake.

Main-net

The primary network where real cryptocurrency transactions are processed and recorded.

Margin Call

Occurs when an investor's margin account falls below the required minimum, requiring them to add more funds or assets.

Margin Trading

Trading using borrowed funds to increase the potential return on investment.

Market Capitalization (Market Cap)

In crypto, it's calculated by multiplying the total supply of a cryptocurrency by its current price.

Market Maker

A participant who creates buy and sell orders to provide liquidity in the market.

Market Order / Market Buy / Market Sell

An order to buy or sell a cryptocurrency at the best available price in the current market.

Market Taker

Someone who buys or sells using existing market orders.

Master-nodes

Nodes responsible for processing blockchain transactions, receiving rewards when a block is mined.

Mem-pool

The collection of unconfirmed transactions waiting to be added to a blockchain.

Merkle Tree

A cryptographic structure where data is hashed and grouped in a way that allows quick verification of data integrity.

Metaverse

A virtual world where users interact in a computer-generated environment.

Micro-Bitcoin (UBTC)

One millionth of a Bitcoin, or 0.000001 BTC, often confused with a Bitcoin fork.

Microtransaction

Small payments made for digital goods or services, often used in gaming.

Mineable

A cryptocurrency that can be mined by contributing computational power to the network.

Miners

Participants who contribute computational power to verify and add transactions to the blockchain.

Mining

The process of validating transactions and creating new blocks on a blockchain.

Mining Contract

Also known as cloud mining, where users invest in mining capacity online.

Mining Pool

A group of miners combining their resources to increase mining power and share block rewards.

Mining Reward

The reward given to miners for using their computing power to process transactions on the blockchain.

Mining Rig

A specialized piece of hardware built for mining cryptocurrencies.

Mnemonic Phrase

Also known as a seed phrase, it's a list of words used to access or recover your cryptocurrency wallet.

Mnemonics

Memory aids, like letters or associations, that help recall information. In crypto, it refers to mnemonic phrases.

Money Printer Go BRRR

A meme describing the excessive money printing by the U.S. Federal Reserve during the COVID-19 pandemic to support the financial markets.

Moon

Crypto slang for when a coin's price skyrockets. When it peaks, it's said to be "mooning."

Mt. Gox

One of the earliest platforms for fiat-to-Bitcoin exchanges, which later became infamous for its collapse.

Multi-signal (multi-signature)

A wallet requiring more than one key to authorize a transaction, adding an extra layer of security.

Node

A computer in the blockchain network that holds a full, updated copy of the blockchain.

Nonce

Short for "number only used once," it's critical in verifying Bitcoin transactions.

Non-custodial

A wallet where the user fully controls their private keys, without third-party management.

Non-Fungible Tokens (NFTs)

Unique tokens on the Ethereum blockchain (ERC-721) that represent collectible assets with individual value.

Off-chain

Transactions that occur outside the blockchain, usually for faster processing.

Offline Staking

Staking cryptocurrencies without having to stay connected to the blockchain.

Open/Close

The price a cryptocurrency starts and ends at during a specific time period, such as the beginning and end of a day.

Open Source

Software that is publicly available for anyone to study, modify, or distribute.

OPML (Optimistic Machine Learning)

A machine learning system using optimistic verification and fraud proofs to handle large models efficiently.

Option

A financial contract giving the buyer the right, but not the obligation, to buy or sell an asset at a set price and time.

Oracles

Services that bring real-world data to blockchains and smart contracts for verification and execution.

Order Book

A digital list of all buy and sell orders on a crypto exchange.

Over The Counter (OTC)

Cryptocurrency trades made directly between two parties, outside of a formal exchange.

Pay-Per-Last N Shares (PPLNS)

A mining pool payment system where miners are only paid once a block is discovered.

Pay-Per-Share (PPS)

A mining payment system where miners are compensated for each valid share they contribute.

Peer-to-Peer (P2P)

A communication system where users interact directly without a central authority.

Permissioned Blockchain

A private blockchain where node participation is restricted and requires authorization.

PFP

Can mean "profile pic" or "picture for proof."

Ponzi Scheme

A fraudulent investment scheme where returns to older investors are paid using the funds of new investors.

Portfolio

A collection of all the cryptocurrencies you hold in one place.

Pre-sale

An exclusive token sale that occurs before a public Initial Coin Offering (ICO).

Privacy Coins

Cryptocurrencies designed to ensure transaction anonymity and user privacy.

Private Keys

The unique alphanumeric code that grants access to your cryptocurrency for transactions.

Proof-of-Authority (POA)

A consensus algorithm where block validation is based on identity and reputation.

Proof-of-Burn (POB)

A consensus method where validators destroy tokens to earn the right to mine a block.

Proof-of-Developer (POD)

A way to vouch for a project's credibility by verifying the identity of its developers.

Proof-of-Stake (POS)

A consensus algorithm where block validators are chosen based on the amount of cryptocurrency they have locked in the system.

Proof-of-Work (PoW)

A consensus mechanism where blocks are validated by solving complex mathematical problems.

Protocol

The set of rules that all participants in a blockchain network must follow for communication and validation.

Public Blockchain

A decentralized, open-source blockchain where anyone can participate.

Public Keys

The alphanumeric code used as a public address to receive cryptocurrency.

Pump and Dump Scheme

A market manipulation tactic where a group inflates an asset's price, then sells off their holdings for profit, causing a price crash.

QR Code

Short for "Quick Response Code," it's a scannable image that stores up to 3KB of data, often used in crypto for payments and transfers.

Reddit r/Cryptocurrency Moon

Moons are rewards given to users for their contributions to the r/Cryptocurrency community on Reddit.

REKT

Slang for "wrecked," typically describing a trade that resulted in heavy losses.

Relative Strength Index (RSI)

A popular technical analysis tool that measures if an asset is overbought or oversold by charting past price movements. RSI values range from 0-100, with <30 indicating oversold and >70 indicating overbought conditions.

Replay Attack

A network attack where valid data is intercepted and resent to trick the recipient into performing actions they didn't intend.

Ring Signature

A digital signature performed by a group, where it's impossible to determine which member's key was used, providing anonymity.

ROI (Return on Investment)

The ratio of net profit to the cost of an investment, showing the profitability of the investment.

Rug Pull

When liquidity is suddenly removed from a project, causing the token's price to collapse.

Salt (Cryptography)

A random value added to a password or passphrase to make its hash more secure, protecting it from easy cracking.

Satoshi

The smallest divisible unit of Bitcoin, where 1 Bitcoin equals 100 million SATOSHIS.

Satoshi Nakamoto

The pseudonym used by the creator of Bitcoin, whose identity remains unknown.

SCRYPT

A memory-intensive hashing algorithm used in Proof-of-Work mining protocols.

Second-Layer Solutions

Frameworks built on top of blockchains to improve transaction speed and scalability.

Secure Asset Fund for Users (SAFU)

A reserve fund set up by Binance to compensate users in case of catastrophic events, like hacks.

Securities and Exchange Commission (SEC)

A U.S. agency that regulates securities markets and enforces federal securities laws.

Seed

A sequence of 12-24 random words used to generate a private key and access a cryptocurrency wallet.

Segregated Witness (SEGWIT)

A Bitcoin protocol update designed to improve scalability by separating transaction signatures from the transaction data.

Sell Wall

A large sell order at a specific price that creates resistance in the order book, preventing the price from rising easily.

SHA-256

A cryptographic algorithm that generates a 64-character hash, part of the SHA-2 family used in Bitcoin mining.

Sharding

A method of splitting a blockchain's data into smaller pieces to improve speed and scalability.

Shilling

The act of promoting a cryptocurrency under false pretenses, often for personal gain.

SHITCOIN

A derogatory term for a cryptocurrency that has little to no value or purpose.

Side Chain

A separate blockchain that runs parallel to a primary blockchain, allowing for more flexibility.

Sim Swapping

A hacking tactic where someone takes over a victim's phone number to bypass two-factor authentication and access accounts.

Smart Contracts

Self-executing contracts coded on the blockchain that run automatically when predefined conditions are met.

Soft Cap

The minimum fundraising goal set by a cryptocurrency project during an ICO.

Soft Fork

A backward-compatible update to a blockchain's protocol that allows old nodes to recognize new transactions.

Software Development Kit (SDK)

A package of tools that helps developers create software for specific devices or operating systems.

Solidity

An object-oriented programming language used to write smart contracts on Ethereum and other blockchain platforms.

SOLO STAKER

A user who stakes their own coins to participate in Proof-of-Stake mining without delegating to others.

Stablecoin

A cryptocurrency that's pegged to a stable asset like a fiat currency or commodity, designed to minimize price volatility.

Staking

Locking in tokens to support the operation of a Proof-of-Stake network, earning rewards in return.

Stale Block

A block that was mined but not included in the main blockchain because another block was added first.

State Channel

An off-chain transaction method that reduces congestion and allows faster processing of transactions.

STO (Security Token Offering)

A fundraising event where investors buy tokenized securities that represent ownership in real-world assets.

Stop-loss Order

A trading order that automatically sells an asset if its price falls below a set threshold to limit losses.

SUPER STAKER

A full node on the QTUM blockchain that offers staking services for delegated addresses, taking a small cut of the block reward.

Tangle

IOTA's unique ledger system that uses a Directed Acyclic Graph (DAG) instead of traditional blockchain technology.

TESTNET

A testing environment for blockchain developers to try new features without affecting the main blockchain.

Ticker

An abbreviation representing a cryptocurrency or asset, used as its symbol for trading.

Token

A digital asset issued by a blockchain project, representing value, utility, or governance rights within the network.

Token Burn

The process of permanently removing tokens from circulation to reduce supply and potentially increase value.

Token Generation Event (TGE)

The moment when new tokens are created and distributed to users, typically during an ICO or another fundraising event.

Total Supply

The total number of tokens or coins that will ever exist for a cryptocurrency.

Total Value Locked (TVL)

The total amount of assets staked or locked into a DeFi protocol.

Trading Volume

The total amount of a cryptocurrency that has been traded over a specific period, usually 24 hours.

Transaction Fee

The payment required to process a transaction on the blockchain, paid to miners or validators.

Transactions Per Second (TPS)

The number of transactions a blockchain can process per second.

Trustless

A system where all actions are verifiable on the blockchain, removing the need to trust any party.

Unspent Transaction Output (UTXO)

Coins in a wallet that haven't been spent yet. UTXOs represent the crypto you still hold in your wallet.

UTC Time

Short for "Universal Time Coordinated," it's the same as Greenwich Mean Time (GMT).

Utility Token

Cryptocurrency tokens that serve specific purposes within a network, beyond just being used for transactions or investments.

Validator

A participant in a Proof of Stake blockchain who signs blocks and has staked a significant number of tokens on the network.

Variable Buy/Sell Tax

A flexible on-chain tax rate for buy/sell transactions, which contract owners can adjust.

Venture Capital

Funds invested in a company that requires large capital to get started.

Virtual AMM (VAMM)

A virtual version of an Automated Market Maker (AMM) without an actual asset pool.

Wallet

Software that stores your cryptocurrencies and lets you send and receive them.

Wallet Address

The unique address where cryptocurrencies are stored, sent, or received.

Wash Trade

A trading strategy where one-party trades back and forth with themselves to artificially inflate trading volume.

Watchlist

A custom list of assets you monitor for changes or activity.

Web3 Wallet

A wallet designed for interacting with decentralized apps (DAPPS) in Web 3.0.

Cryptocurrency

Wei

The smallest unit of Ether, with 1 Ether equaling 1,000,000,000,000,000,000 Wei.

Whale

Someone who owns a massive amount of cryptocurrency and can influence market prices.

When Lambo

A phrase investor use when asking when their investment will grow enough to buy a Lamborghini.

When Moon

A term used by investors to ask when a coin's price will reach its peak.

Whitelist

A list of approved participants allowed to join a token sale (like an ICO or IEO).

Whitepaper

A document outlining a project, explaining an issue and proposing a solution.

Yield Farming

Earning interest or rewards by depositing cryptocurrency into a DeFi protocol.

YTD

Stands for "Year-to-date."

Zero Confirmation Transaction

Another term for an unconfirmed transaction.

Zero Knowledge Proof

A cryptographic method where two parties can verify something without revealing the actual information.

ZK-SNARKS

A cryptographic protocol allowing someone to prove possession of information without revealing it or requiring interaction between parties.

ZKML (Zero-Knowledge Machine Learning)

Combines zero-knowledge proofs with machine learning to ensure privacy in ML computations.

ZKORACLE

An advanced blockchain oracle that uses zero-knowledge proofs to securely verify external data without revealing the data itself.

Why Crypto is the future of money today?

We're on the brink of a new way of handling money that's set to shake things up using various technologies. The old ways of doing things—like getting cash from ATMs, going to banks for loans, or shopping at department stores—are fading fast. Nowadays, most financial transactions happen online, a trend that really took off during the COVID-19 pandemic. More and more, the future of money is happening in the digital world, through our phones and laptops.

But there's even more to come. Cryptocurrencies and new, advanced financial technologies are changing how we think about money and are putting pressure on traditional banks and financial systems. 2021 was a major turning point for finance, and 2022 looks set to bring even more changes.

Cryptocurrency

ZDNet is diving into two key areas that are shaping the future of money: blockchain and fintech innovations.

Cryptocurrency is basically digital money secured by cryptography, which means it uses complex math to keep transactions safe, all handled on a tech called blockchain. Take Bitcoin, for example – it was the first decentralized cryptocurrency, created in 2009, and is still the most well-known with a huge market cap of around $787 billion as of early January 2022. While many people have heard of Bitcoin, few actually understand it. Here's a key thing: Bitcoin and blockchain aren't the same. Blockchain is like a shared, unchangeable record that links encrypted blocks of transaction data in a secure network. Each cryptocurrency, like Bitcoin, has its own unique blockchain to track its transactions.

Cryptocurrency

Right now, there are approximately over 17,000 different cryptocurrencies out there. Bitcoin is the largest, and the second biggest is Ether, which, along with all cryptocurrencies except Bitcoin, runs on the Ethereum blockchain. Altogether, cryptocurrencies are estimated to be worth around $3 trillion.

However, the value of Bitcoin and other cryptos took a hit this year as the Federal Reserve adopted a stricter stance on its monetary policy, reducing its bond holdings and signaling upcoming interest rate hikes. Even though cryptos operate independently from central banks and governments, they're still impacted by the global financial market's ups and downs.

Apart from being volatile, cryptocurrencies remain controversial. Critics argue that since they aren't tied to a regulated central bank or government,

Cryptocurrency

they're tougher—if not impossible—to oversee. This lack of regulation has made Bitcoin and other cryptos attractive for those looking to launder money, purchase illegal items, or bypass financial controls.

A top analyst AVIVAH LITAN, and VP at Gartner, explained to ZDNet that within three to five years, cryptocurrencies will start being used for retail payments. Right now, and over the next few years, we're seeing investors get into crypto as a way to protect against inflation or as a gold alternative. But it's still highly volatile—Bitcoin, for instance, is currently valued at around $41,197, a big drop from its peak of $88,243 on November 20, 2021.

Despite the ups and downs, investors and companies aren't shying away from crypto's potential. It's not all about price speculation, either. Some investors and companies are diving into decentralized finance, or DeFi, to explore new finance methods. As LITAN pointed out, companies—and even hedge funds—are increasingly putting money into crypto.

To support these companies, banks are stepping in as digital asset custodians, and it's happening globally, not just in the U.S. LITAN noted that institutional finance is starting to show interest in DeFi. Currently, cryptocurrency makes up about 0.08% of assets, and some surveys suggest that hedge funds could hold up to 8% of their assets in crypto within five years.

Cracking down on crypto scams and misuse is key to building trust in the market. Gartner predicts that by 2025, successful cryptocurrency thefts and ransomware payouts will drop by 32% because criminals are finding it harder to move and cash out funds from blockchain networks. This is especially good news considering crypto crimes—mostly scams and thefts—reached a record $17 billion in 2021, up from $8.9 billion the previous year, according to CHAINALYSIS. New scams, like "rug pulls" where developers make a project seem legit and then vanish with investors' cash, have been on the rise. Also, North Korean hackers scored nearly $451 million in digital assets in 2021 after several attacks on investment firms and exchanges.

Still, despite crypto's big growth in 2021, there's a silver lining: illegal activity hit an all-time low. CHAINALYSIS reported that just 0.15% of crypto transactions involved criminal addresses in 2021, down from 0.62% in 2020.

Blockchain is also transforming loyalty rewards programs. For years, loyalty programs frustrated customers with rigid conditions and limits on using points. Many customers walked away, feeling it wasn't worth it. But with online shopping taking over, retailers are turning to blockchain to manage transactions and improve customer experience by adding flexibility, transparency, and a clearer value system.

There's a lot of talk about what the "metaverse" might look like—a virtual reality-driven Web where the physical and digital worlds blend together. Even though nobody's sure exactly how it'll take shape, one thing's clear: the metaverse is going to be a fully functional marketplace where users can move freely as digital versions of themselves and shop in virtual stores.

Though it's not controlled by any single company—big names like Google, Microsoft, and Samsung are also in the game—Facebook (now Meta) has gone all-in, even rebranding itself to focus on this vision. Meta describes its version of the metaverse as a collection of virtual spaces where people can meet, work, play, shop, and create together.

There's a mix of excitement and skepticism around the metaverse, especially with talk of how it might bring together shopping and crypto. GARTNER'S LITAN thinks that as DeFi grows, consumers will soon start using digital currencies in the metaverse. She believes platforms like Meta, NFTs, and play-to-earn games will introduce users to spending virtual currency.

Cryptocurrency

BEST TIMING TO INVEST IN CRYPTO

Simon Chandler is a journalist based in London. He writes about technology, markets and politics, and has bylines for *Forbes, Digital Trends, CCN, Wired, TechCrunch,* the *Verge,* the *Sun,* the *New Internationalist,* and *Truth-Out,* among many others.

According to **Simon Chandler |Sep 20, 2024**

"In a market defined by volatility and uncertainty, investors have a tendency to look for regularities, averages and patterns wherever they can find them. This is entirely understandable, especially when the gains and losses in crypto tend to exceed those witnessed in more conventional markets. And it's especially understandable in 2022, when cryptocurrency losses have outnumbered gains, exposing traders to greater risks than in other years.

One area in which (some) investors look for regularities is in the timing of cryptocurrency movements. Yes, there's a wealth of data available on this subject, from month-by-month return percentages for the bitcoin price, to heat maps on Ethereum gas fees by the hour. This article collates such data into a global picture, providing some insight into the best time, days and months of the year to buy crypto.

Cryptocurrency

1 The Best Months for Crypto Investment

Starting with the biggest unit of time (other than years themselves, which aren't significant), an inspection of the best months of the year to buy crypto yields some intriguing results.

A chart of the best month for crypto investments

Bitcoin gains/losses per month since 2009. Source: bitcoinmonthlyreturn.com

As the chart above shows, 2022 has been the worst year for monthly BTC gains since 2018, with seven months in the red so far (compared to nine for 2018).

With regards to how the months themselves fare, the chart can be parsed in one of two ways. Firstly, it shows average returns and total returns (since 2009) for each month, which can be presented in the following way:

- November – average gains: 39.21%; total gains: 548.87%

- April – average gains: 36.01%; total gains: 504.16%

- October – average gains: 26.79%; total gains: 375.04%

- May – average gains: 19.59%; total gains: 274.19%

- February – average gains: 13.42%; total gains: 187.83%

- December – average gains: 11.46%; total gains: 160.37%

- March – average gains: 8.2%; total gains: 114.74%

- July – average gains: 8.18%; total gains: 114.5%

- January – average gains: 7.59%; total gains: 106.25%

- June – average gains: 7.46%; total gains: 104.4%

- August – average gains: 0.73%; total gains: 10.28%

- September – average gains: -5.01%; total gains: -70.08%

A few things can be gleaned from such figures. To begin with, if a trader wants to increase the probability of making a profit, they may want to focus their buying on the October/November and April/May periods, which have historically posted the biggest average monthly returns for bitcoin.

Of course, investors need to be mindful that they would want to buy crypto just before these periods, so that they maximize their potential gains. For example, the data shows that September has historically been the worst month on record for bitcoin gains, so a savvy investor might want to wait until the end of September and then make a purchase, just in time for the potential increases October and November could bring.

In terms of the optimum time of the month for purchases, bitcoin's price chart reveals that it's often the start of the month (i.e. the first ten days or so) that tend to bring the bulk of the gains. This is particularly the case with its action in 2021, which was a very bullish year for the cryptocurrency, bringing multiple rallies.

Bitcoin's price chart for 2021. Source: COINGECKO

Of course, some may say that this data is really only valid for bitcoin, and not for other cryptocurrencies. However, most cryptocurrencies are heavily correlated with BTC, so it can still be taken as an indication of what coins such as Ethereum and ripple may also do on any given month of the year.

2 Best Days of the Month to Buy Crypto, and Times of the Day

Turning to specific days, there isn't the kind of price data that ranks each day according to average returns since the birth of bitcoin/cryptocurrency. Nonetheless, there are various pieces of evidence and data that do offer some valuable insights.

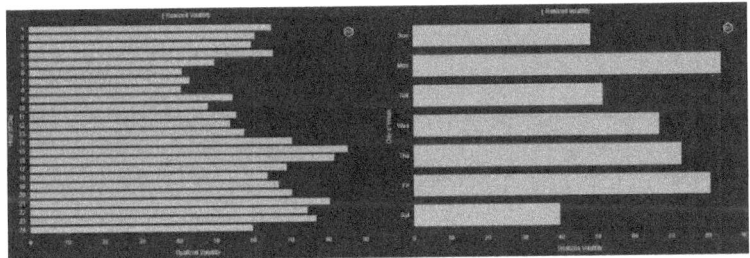

Average realized bitcoin volatility per hour of the day (left), and per day of the week (right). Source: Genesis Volatility/Amber-data

For example, bitcoin volatility data for each day shows that the weekends generally aren't great for traders looking to make a quick profit. Instead, they may prefer to look at either Monday or Thursday/Friday, where bigger movements tend to be clustered. This works both ways though, so it may also increase the risk of a fall, particularly in more bearish years.

The volatility data above is also supported by average Ethereum gas prices, which again shows less activity on weekends, although in this case things heat up most on Tuesdays and Wednesdays. What this implies is that, if you're looking to day trade or for short-term action, doing it on Saturday or Sunday is not really a good idea.

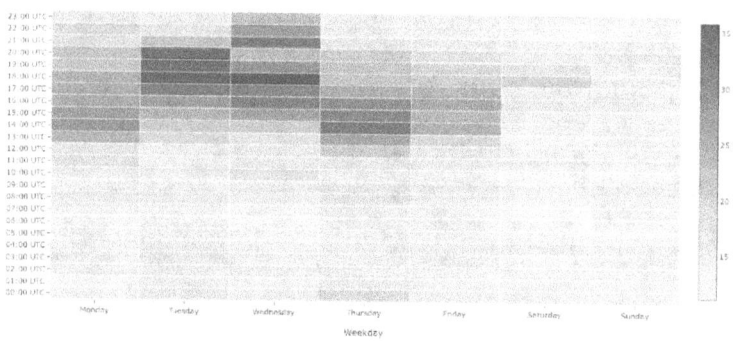

Source: Any-block Analytics

What the above two charts also show is times of day with the highest volatility/gas prices, and what's interesting is that they both show greater activity later in the day. For example, in both cases the busy periods tend to be between 3:00 pm UTC (or 10:00 am Eastern Time, 7:00 am Pacific) and 9pm UTC (4pm Eastern, 1pm Pacific). So, anyone assuming that the market is more likely to move up rather than down — and who wants to make a quick buck — is advised to time moves just before this window of opportunity.

3 Warnings

Almost needless to say, 'timing' is mostly irrelevant for investors playing a long-term game, at least with regards to days and hours. Instead, many long-term holders may be better off simply adopting a dollar cost averaging approach, buying a little of their desired cryptocurrency each month. Such an approach tends to 'average out' volatility over the longer term, although short-term traders who live for volatility may not appreciate this.

Also, it has to be said that, while the data above covers bitcoin/cryptocurrency history up until the present day, there's no guarantee that the future will resemble the past. So even though the weekends aren't great for volatility, and even though November has historically been the best month for bitcoin returns, this needn't be the case in the coming years.

As such, going long in the fullest sense of the term and using dollar cost averaging remains the way to go for most retail investors."

How to Buy Cryptocurrencies Today

If you're looking to buy crypto to use for purchases, you'll need to head over to a cryptocurrency exchange. These exchanges let you buy and sell crypto from other users at the going market rate, much like a stock exchange. Once you've bought your crypto, you'll need to move it to a digital wallet or use a service like Coinbase to store it safely.

If your goal is just to invest in cryptocurrency, you might be able to do that through a broker. For example, platforms like Robinhood let you invest in Bitcoin and other cryptos, but you can't withdraw them for spending. You can also invest in crypto through exchange-traded funds (ETFs), which give you exposure to the crypto market without needing your own wallet. For instance, by May 2024, investors can hold Bitcoin futures ETFs or Ether spot shares, which have been approved by the SEC.

Written by Rickie Houston and

Tessa Campbell; edited by SARAH SILBERT

Sep 30, 2024, 2:30 PM GMT+1

"A crypto exchange is a platform dedicated to facilitating the trading of cryptocurrency. Each exchange has its own rules for buying, selling, and trading cryptocurrency.

The best exchange for you depends on your needs, but beginners should look for exchanges that offer simple web and mobile interfaces, educational resources, and readily available customer support.

It is worth keeping in mind that while there is a large number of such marketplaces, there is a short list of organizations you should consider if you are seeking to use one of the best crypto exchanges out there.

Cryptocurrency

Depending on the crypto exchange, you can trade one cryptocurrency for another, or exchange fiat money (like the U.S. dollar) for cryptocurrency, or vice versa. Prices are based on daily market rates. **Quick tip:** With crypto also comes stablecoins and non-fungible tokens (NFTs). Stablecoins are backed by fiat currencies like the US Dollar to stabilize their value (if it's backed by dollars, you can usually redeem one stablecoin for $1). NFTs, however, are unique, art-or-collectible-associated tokens that can't be exchanged for other tokens.

It should be noted that not every exchange offers every cryptocurrency. But here are several exchanges and brokerages that do:

Cryptocurrency

Exchange/broker	Features
Kraken	Global support, 100+ cryptocurrencies, margin and futures trading, staking, and institutional services
Coinbase	200+ crypto assets, wallet storage, educational resources, Coinbase Card (crypto-linked Visa debit card), non-fungible token (NFT) marketplace, institutional services, crypto-backed loans
Binance.US	More than 100 cryptocurrencies, staking rewards, over-the-counter trading, and institutional services

There are both centralized and decentralized exchanges. The most prominent exchanges, for example Coinbase and Kraken, are centralized, whereas decentralized exchanges are peer-to-peer (P2P) marketplaces where transactions take place directly between users.

Decentralized exchanges rely on smart contracts, which ensure that transactions take place as long as specific requirements are fulfilled.

While decentralized exchanges have seen increasing usage over time, centralized exchanges still see far more activity.

4 Traditional brokers

Interested parties can also purchase digital currencies through traditional brokers. Traditional online brokerages that offer cryptocurrencies are few, but more options are becoming available for crypto-oriented traders.

Online brokerages usually don't offer as many cryptocurrencies as crypto exchanges (nor do they provide interest-earning account perks like staking).

One example of a broker that offers these digital assets IS ETORO USA, which offers trading in more than 20 cryptocurrencies.

Another example is Robinhood, which currently offers no-commission cryptocurrency trades. Users can buy and sell 15 different digital currencies through this platform.

Interactive Brokers offers digital currency trading, although it only allows investors to trade four cryptocurrencies, specifically bitcoin, Ethereum, LITECOIN and bitcoin cash. This platform offers low commissions for such transactions, which can be as little as 0.12% to 0.18% of the value of the asset traded.

You should choose a broker if you're looking to trade a variety of asset types under the same roof. TRADESTATION offers cryptocurrencies in addition to its selection of stocks, ETFs, options, bonds, and mutual funds.

5 Payment apps

Several payment apps give their users the ability to purchase cryptocurrencies. These software programs can offer easy access to digital assets.

In recent years, payment services like PayPal, Cash App, and Venmo, all expanded their accepted payment options, allowing users to buy, sell, or hold cryptocurrencies like bitcoin. Every one of these services has an app that users can access to make transactions.

6 Bitcoin ATMs

Bitcoin ATMs provide an easy way for interested parties to buy and sell the digital currency. As of January 1, 2024, there were more than 30,000 of these machines worldwide, according to Statista figures.

These machines offer users a straightforward way to purchase bitcoin using more traditional payment methods like cash and bank cards. These machines frequently leverage two-factor authentication, which requires multiple steps to verify a user, to help ensure the security of transactions.

Users should keep in mind that the fees associated with bitcoin ATMs can be high, according to figures provided by the Federal Reserve Bank of Kansas City, with interested parties often paying total fees of 20%.

7 Peer-to-peer (P2P) marketplaces

As stated earlier, decentralized exchanges provide crypto investors with P2P marketplaces where they can make transactions involving digital currencies.

These platforms depend on smart contracts to make sure that transactions take place.

Investors might take an interest in decentralized exchanges because transaction participants are not required to disclose their private keys like they would when using a centralized exchange.

Further, decentralized exchanges can charge low fees.

Decentralized exchanges also don't hold investor funds, making them less appealing to hackers.

8 Fees and commissions

Keep in mind that the total fees and commissions associated with trading platforms can vary quite a bit. Many exchanges charge not only trading fees, but also fees for deposits and withdrawals. Fortunately, there are many different exchanges, platforms and apps you can use to purchase cryptocurrency. This competition may place downward pressure on total fees.

9 Security

When evaluating different platforms, the measures they use to ensure the security of their users is a major consideration. Two-factor authentication is common. Some exchanges put their cryptocurrency into cold storage, meaning that it is held offline, helping eliminate much of the risk that digital currencies will be compromised as a result of a hack.

In addition, some exchanges pay for insurance to help safeguard their users. Coinbase, for example, has crime insurance. "Coinbase carries crime insurance that protects a portion of digital currencies held across our storage systems against losses from theft, including cybersecurity breaches," the Coinbase website states.

"However, our policy does not cover any losses resulting from unauthorized access to your personal Coinbase or Coinbase Pro account(s) due to a breach or loss of your credentials," it adds.

Investors should keep in mind that cryptocurrency exchanges are not insured by the Federal Deposit Insurance Corporation, which provides insurance for banks.

10 Available cryptocurrencies

Bitcoin, the world's most well-known cryptocurrency, can be purchased through many different mediums. Many exchanges offer far more than bitcoin, with some of these marketplaces offering trading of hundreds of cryptocurrencies.

The easiest way to determine which cryptocurrencies a platform, exchange or app offers is to simply peruse its website.

11 Reputation and user experience

As always, investors should perform thorough due diligence before using any platform, exploring its reputation and reviews left by users. Fortunately, there is a wealth of information on different exchanges that interested parties can access online.

Coinbase, in particular, has a reputation of being a safe exchange, although this organization is not without security breaches. In 2021, this platform suffered a hack that resulted in at least 6,000 users losing funds.

12 Types of wallets

Cryptocurrency users frequently use wallets to hold the private keys they need to access their digital assets. These wallets can come in many forms, ranging from software wallets to hardware devices specifically designed to retain this information.

Technically, a user can write their private keys on a piece of paper, or alternatively, they can type them up using a word processor and print them out. While this may seem basic, it at least eliminates the risk of someone accessing one's private keys through the internet.

Hardware wallets, for example thumb drives, are also secure, as they only connect to computers (like desktop and laptop devices) when necessary.

There are several variables to consider for investors who are trying to determine how to choose a crypto wallet.

When evaluating different crypto wallets, keep in mind that the amount of cryptocurrency you have plays a key role. If you only have a small amount invested, paying for expensive hardware doesn't make sense. However, if you have a significant amount of money in cryptocurrency, paying for more elaborate security measures may seem perfectly reasonable.

Quick tip: If your exchange doesn't offer a wallet, you may need to set up one with a personal wallet service. There are several different types of providers that may charge fees depending on whether it's a hot or cold wallet. For example, cold wallets always generally charge fees, while hot wallets generally don't.

13 Importance of security

Investors who want to keep their cryptocurrency secure can benefit from using strong passwords.

For example, a user might want to craft a password that has many different characters, including letters, numbers and symbols.

Two-factor authentication can go a long way toward safeguarding one's digital currency assets. While it may seem inconvenient by taking more time, using multiple steps to verify your identity may be well worth it in the grand scheme of things.

14 Transferring your crypto

Another strategy that many investors use to safeguard their cryptocurrency is buying it on exchanges and then transferring it to one or more wallets. Exchanges can hold very substantial amounts of cryptocurrency, making them compelling targets for hackers.

By moving their digital currency from exchanges to digital wallets, investors can transfer these assets to a far less visible place. Further, by sending cryptocurrencies to a hardware wallet, an investor can take their assets offline and make them far more secure.

Making your first crypto purchase: Step-by-step instructions

1. Choose a crypto provider

Start by setting up an account through a platform that allows you to purchase cryptocurrencies, such as the well-known exchange Coinbase.

To initiate this process, you will need to be at least 18 years of age and have access to a valid government ID you can use to confirm your identity, a computer or smartphone you can use to access Coinbase, and updated software. More specifically, using this exchange to make transactions will require you to have the latest version of the Coinbase app or the largest version of your browser (Coinbase recommends that interested parties use Google Chrome).

2. Set up a crypto-trading account

Once you have put these resources together, you can set up an account. Coinbase suggests that you do this either through the app (if using a smartphone) or through a browser (if you are using a computer). Coinbase recommends that potential users refrain from setting up accounts through the browser on their phone.

Setting up an account requires you to enter some basic information (legal name, the state where you reside, email address and a password) and then indicate that you agree to both the company's User Agreement and Privacy Policy. Once you have reviewed these, you click on "SIGN UP" if using a mobile device or "Create account" if using a computer.

3. Verify crypto account

After this, Coinbase may send you a message designed to verify your email address. If you receive this, it will come from no-reply@coinbase.com, and all you have to do is click on "Verify Email Address," which will in turn bring you to the Coinbase website where you can log in using your email address and password.

You will need to verify a phone number you wish to associate with your account, which requires signing in to your Coinbase account and then receiving a code sent to your phone via SMS, which you will, in turn, use to confirm your number with the exchange.

4. Provide personal information

After that, you enter personal information as displayed on your government ID. Keep in mind that all the information needs to match up with the form of identification, as you will be required to submit it to Coinbase as part of the verification process.

You will need to provide some more information left off an ID, including your social security number and occupation, and then you will need to answer some basic questions like "What do you use Coinbase for?" and "What is your source of funds?"

Once you have completed the aforementioned step, you will have finished the application process. Assuming Coinbase approves your account, you will need to verify your identity by submitting documentation and then link a payment method you will use to fund your account.

5. Fund your crypto account

Next, you will need to fund your account, which you can do using many different methods. The various means you can use to fund your account will vary based on your jurisdiction, but in the U.S., the methods include your bank account, a debit card, Google Pay and PayPal.

6. Purchase cryptocurrencies

Once you have funded your account, you can purchase a cryptocurrency by signing in to Coinbase.com, going to Buy/Sell, selecting a digital currency from the Buy tab, specifying the amount of the cryptocurrency you want to purchase, singling out a payment method, selecting Preview Buy so you can verify the details of your transaction, and, assuming the details reflect the exact purchase you want to make, clicking Buy Now."

CONCLUSION

In summary, the crypto market is a thrilling space with big growth potential in the next few years. Key drivers for crypto's growth by 2025 will be market trends, new tech developments, government regulations, and the state of the economy.

Some of the top cryptos that could see major gains by 2025 include Bitcoin, Ethereum, Ripple, CARDANO, AND POLKADOT.

When diving into crypto investments, it's crucial to do thorough research and be aware of the risks involved.

All in all, there are plenty of exciting opportunities in crypto over the next five years that investors shouldn't miss out on.

Cryptocurrency

As we look forward, the crypto landscape is likely to keep evolving with new projects, partnerships, and innovations, giving investors plenty to keep an eye on. With decentralized finance (DeFi) gaining traction and blockchain technology advancing, we're likely to see more real-world applications and increased adoption, which can further boost the value and utility of cryptocurrencies.

Additionally, as regulation around crypto becomes clearer, more traditional investors and institutions are expected to enter the space, bringing stability and growth. This means there could be more options for both everyday investors and big players to get involved in different ways, from staking and lending to NFTs and metaverse projects.

For anyone considering crypto, the next few years will be an exciting time, with lots of potential for growth—but it's always important to stay informed,

Cryptocurrency

think long-term, and remember that the crypto market can be unpredictable.

www.ingramcontent.com/pod-product-compliance
Lightning Source LLC
Chambersburg PA
CBHW052209220526
45471CB00004B/1888